Tracy L. Williams

However, when He, the Spirit of Truth, is come, He will guide you into all truth; for He shall not speak from Himself, but whatsoever He shall hear, that shall He speak; and He will show you things to come. He shall glorify Me, for He shall receive of Mine, and shall show it unto you.

~John 16:13, 14 NKJV

14 Reasons to Pray in the Holy Spirit

Tracy L. Williams

I DEDICATE THIS BOOK TO THE CONTINUED WISDOM OF THE HOLY SPIRIT - THAT JESUS BE GLORIFIED, AND CHRIST BE MAGNIFIED.

I ALSO GIVE LOVE AND SPECIAL THANKS TO MY HUSBAND AND BEST FRIEND, DR. JUAN FOR HIS LOVE AND LEADERSHIP IN OUR FAMILY AND MINISTRY.

14 Reasons to Pray in the Holy Spirit

© 2018 TLW Publications
Published by TLW Publications
P.O. Box 1413
Claremont, CA 91711 - 1413

First edition print October 2018
Second edition print June 2019

Printed in the United States of America

All rights reserved. No part of this book may be reproduced, scanned, or distributed in any printed or electronic form without permission by the author, Tracy L. Williams and publisher, TLW Publications.

ISBN-13: 978-0-9894241-5-8 (Paperback)
ISBN: 978-0-9894241-6-5 (eBook / ePub)

Unless otherwise indicated:
Scripture quotations taken from THE AMPLIFIED BIBLE, Copyright © 1954, 1958, 1962, 1964, 1965, 1987 by The Lockman Foundation. All rights reserved. Used by permission. Scripture taken from the New King James Version. copyright©1982 by Thomas Nelson, Inc. Used by permission. All rights reserved.

Photo credits: All images are original photos taken during travel by the author Tracy L. Williams.
Book design by TLW Publications.
Cover design by Thule – Empire Printing & Publishing

Tracy L. Williams

~EPHESIANS 3:3-5 NKJV

...how that by revelation He made known to me the mystery (as I have briefly written already, **4** by which, when you read, you may understand my knowledge in the mystery of Christ), **5** which in other ages was not made known to the sons of men, as it has now been revealed by the Spirit to His holy apostles and prophets...

Tracy L. Williams

14 Reasons to Pray in the Holy Spirit
...Heaven's Language

Introduction: Understanding – The Baptism with the Holy Spirit	1
#1 - It's a New Language – *Heaven's*	17
#2 - Prayer Is Not to Men but, Directly to God	23
#3 - Mysteries of God are Released	31
#4 - The Wonderful Works of God are Declared	37
#5 - God is Magnified/Glorified	47
#6 - It's Your Spirit Praying	53
#7 - The Fire of God is Released	59
#8 - It's Evidence of the Spirit-Filled Life	65
#9 - It's a Sign for Non-Believers	73
#10 - It's Selfless Intercession	83
#11 - The One Praying is Reminded of What God Said	91
#12 - The One Praying is Personally Edified	97
#13 - The One Praying Receives Most Holy Faith	103
#14 - To Be Perfected in Love	109
Conclusion: Spiritual Warfare is Real	115
Prayer of Repentance	127
Prayer to Receive the Gift of the Holy Spirit	133
The Author's Page	137

14 Reasons to Pray in the Holy Spirit

Tracy L. Williams

**INTRODUCTION: UNDERSTANDING
THE BAPTISM WITH THE HOLY SPIRIT**

...and the Holy Spirit descended on Him in bodily form like a dove, and a voice came from heaven, "You are My Son, My Beloved, in You I am well-pleased and delighted!" When He began His ministry... Luke 3:22-23

14 Reasons to Pray in the Holy Spirit

"In you, I am well pleased." Those words from God are words any person would desire to hear personally when we consider what just took place with Jesus - He was not only water baptized but was baptized with the Holy Spirit. It was not until the Holy Spirit descended on Jesus like a dove that those words were heard from the mouth of God.

When we do not lean to our own understanding, it becomes very clear that this is something followers of Jesus Christ should aspire to attain. Jesus was filled with the Holy Spirit. The Holy Spirit actually descended on Him like a dove. Therefore, if you confess with your mouth the Lord Jesus and believe in your heart that God has raised Him from the dead, you will be saved. The next step is to repent and be baptized (every one of you) in the name of Jesus Christ for the remission of sins, and you will receive the gift of the Holy Spirit (Acts 2:38). When this happens, the Holy Spirit lives in us, just as the Father and Son lives in us because they are ONE.

Jesus answered and said to him, "If anyone loves Me, he will keep My word; and My Father will

love him, and We will come to him and make Our home with him. John 14:23 NKJV

This is the place where many born-again believers remain stuck. Jesus became Lord and Savior when they were born again, but the power to keep Him Lord over and in their lives comes with a greater knowing of the power made available to them through the baptism with the Holy Spirit. After being saved (born-again) we can receive the greater ministry that is given and administered by the Holy Spirit through the believer. There is yet another Source of power made available - power that is considered a vital force; a source of power that is supernatural; a strength that can not be compared to anything in the natural. It is the Holy Spirit – the Spirit and grace of God Himself – Who empowers this power. This power is only for those who believe.

"But there is [a vital force and] a spirit [of intelligence] in man, and the breath of the Almighty gives them understanding." Job 32:8

14 Reasons to Pray in the Holy Spirit

We receive the baptism with the Holy Spirit by faith, just as we receive any other promise from God. It is not automatic. This gift doesn't just come with salvation. Faith activates what God has promised. Our faith to believe and receive the promise of the Holy Spirit grants the Holy Spirit permission to move in our lives and through our bodies. I know this sounds celestial – it is that and more! It's supernatural… it's spiritual… exactly Who God is. God is Spirit, and those who worship Him must worship in spirit and truth (John 4:24 NKJV).

"And, he asked them, 'Did you receive the Holy Spirit when you believed (on Jesus as the Christ)?' And they said, "No, we have not even heard that there is a Holy Spirit." Acts 19:2

In Acts 2:38, Peter said, "Repent. Change your life. Turn to God and be baptized, each of you, in the name of Jesus Christ, so your sins are forgiven. Receive the gift of the Holy Spirit. The promise is targeted to you and your children, but also to all who are far away—whomever, in fact, our Master God invites." In the latter half of the verse it shows that we have a part to do... to receive. We are to receive the gift of the Holy Spirit.

Also, in Mark 16:15-20, Jesus is speaking... "Go into all the world and preach the gospel to all creation. He who has believed [in Me] and has been baptized will be saved [from the penalty of God's wrath and judgment]; but he who has not believed will be condemned. These signs will accompany those who have believed: in My name they will cast out demons, <u>they will speak in new tongues</u>; they will pick up serpents, and if they drink anything deadly, it will not hurt them; they will lay hands on the sick, and they will get well. So then, when the Lord Jesus had spoken to them, He was taken up into heaven and sat down at the right hand of God. And they went out and preached everywhere, while the Lord was working with them and confirming the word by the signs that followed."

It's up to us to receive all that comes with the born-again life. God will allow what we allow. The baptism with the Holy Spirit and speaking in your heavenly language (tongues) is a choice. Whether we are in ministry or not – or if we simply desire a more intimate, deeper relationship with the Lord, praying in the Spirit can keep or get you there.

If ye then, being evil, know how to give good gifts unto your children; how much more shall your heavenly Father give the Holy Spirit to them that ask Him? Luke 11:13 KJV

Therefore, having been exalted to the right hand of God, and having *received* from the Father the promise of the Holy Spirit, He has poured out this [blessing] which you both see and hear. Acts 2:33

Now, I'm not trying to convince anyone of the truth that baptism with the Holy Spirit is the key missing element for the believer. It is not my purpose to debate with one who continues (yet saved) not to experience the fullness of God's presence and His peace, along with the victory they already have over the flesh and the power they have over sin. Nor am I trying to convince someone who has made up their mind concerning this truth due to past teachings or traditions. The person I am ministering to in this book already has an ear to hear what the Spirit of God is speaking to the Church.

God is calling the believers to whom I am ministering, to a deeper, more intimate relationship with Him. This book is for the born-again believer that knows there is more of God yet to experience. The baptism with the Holy Spirit with evidence of speaking in another tongue (the heavenly language) must come by revelation… with the understanding that one can come to a revelation of God's word and what He is saying that will change their lives forever.

"For I want you to know, brethren, that the Gospel which was proclaimed and made known by me is not man's gospel (a human invention, according to or patterned after any human standard). For indeed I did not receive it from man, nor was I taught it, but (it came to me) through a (direct) revelation (given) by Jesus Christ (the Messiah)." Galatians 1:11, 12

14 Reasons to Pray in the Holy Spirit

Jesus started His ministry after He was baptized with the Holy Spirit. We never hear or read that He started His ministry before this divinely, recorded time in the Bible (Luke 11:23). He was doing good works, but when He got Spirit-filled (filled with the Holy Spirit), He began to do great works.

Baptism with the Holy Spirit can take place after salvation or the born-again experience. It is a separate act of faith that the born-again believer prays for and receives. (These prayers are in the back of this book if needed, or if you just want to refresh the anointing). Let me use myself, the author given to steward this book, as an example:

In 2001, I attended a powerful, Sunday church service in a Chicago church called Living Word Christian Center (under the leadership of Dr. Bill Winston). At the end of that service a call was made for those who would like to get saved and make Jesus the Lord of their life. There was also a call for those who desired to return from a backslidden state and rededicate their lives to Christ. I had already received Jesus as my Lord years before, but most definitely was not living in obedience to God's word. I received the call for everything mentioned from the pulpit that day. I used my faith, got up, walked to the altar, and received Jesus into my heart (again) - this time with a heart that was sincere and tired of being tired – a contrite heart and with a made-up mind.

I know, without a doubt that it was at this point that I humbled myself and recognized this call from God was an honor and a privilege (nothing to play with or ignore). I knew my life was truly being saved from death. Only the Lord knows - I most definitely could have been dead before this life changing day. He actually chose me, I wasn't doing God a favor by choosing Him. I had a conviction in my heart that all God had for me was good and I was ready.

You have not chosen Me, but I have chosen you and I have appointed and placed and purposefully planted you, so that you would go and bear fruit and keep on bearing, and that your fruit will remain and be lasting, so that whatever you ask of

the Father in My name [as My representative] He may give to you. John 15:16

I've made note that that was my true day of salvation because inside change immediately began to take place. That same hour I was baptized in the name of Jesus in the baptism pool made available at the ministry. Upon my return from the baptismal pool a minister prayed with me to receive the gift of the Holy Spirit – to be baptized with the Holy Spirit. I believed, and I received, and I began to pray in tongues immediately. It was like it was already in me just waiting to release... which is so true, and also the revelation given in this book. That very week I began my ministry – the Holy Spirit's ministry – now working through me – at the workplace. I knew it was supernatural how God began to use me and speak through me in ways that I had never imagined or experienced before being filled with the Holy Spirit and speaking in my prayer language (tongues).

...for I will give you [skillful] words and wisdom which none of your opponents will be able to resist or refute. Luke 21:15

I was not raised in the church. Over the years I had visited a few Catholic services with family here and there, and also a few Baptist ministries with friends who most definitely wanted me to get saved. Even when I lived in Hollywood I frequented a specific ministry but never sold out (completely surrendered my will) for Jesus' will. Before entering the ministry that day in Chicago I did not have any preconceived thoughts, notions, or teachings that could cloud my mind to the truth that God would have me to receive all that He had for me - to be full of Him and operate boldly out of His power. The same power Jesus operated out of. The same power that raised Jesus from the dead. The same power that raised me from the dead. I never turned back. I received salvation. I was water baptized in Jesus' name, and was spirit-filled; baptized with the Holy Spirit.

14 Reasons to Pray in the Holy Spirit

And if the Spirit of Him who raised Jesus from the dead lives in you, He who raised Christ Jesus from the dead will also give life to your mortal bodies through His Spirit, who lives in you. Romans 8:11

Today I'm still praying boldly and confidently in the Spirit and living a life that lines up with God's word. I've made some mistakes over the years, but I no longer practice sin. Once I was spirit-filled the Holy Spirit had permission to move in my heart and perfect those things that concerned me and my salvation. There was (and yet remains) a greater conviction in my heart to do right and live right. I give all glory to God understanding that it is not by my power or by my might. It is obviously by the Spirit of the living God and a yielded heart. Right now, today, I purpose to keep my heart right, with God and man, to allow a greater flow of the anointing, the ministry of the Holy Spirit, through my life into others. I don't know it all and I'm not the smartest but, by the Spirit of wisdom I was able to choose life... get spirit-filled, baptized with the Holy Spirit, and begin speaking in my prayer language (heavenly language, tongues). I was wise enough to choose LIFE.

"As for me, I baptize you with water because of [your] repentance [that is, because you are willing to change your inner self—your old way of thinking, regret your sin and live a changed life], but He (the Messiah) who is coming after me is mightier [more powerful, more noble] than I, whose sandals I am not worthy to remove [even as His slave]; He will baptize you [who truly repent] with the Holy Spirit and [you who remain unrepentant] with fire (judgment). Matthew 3:11

14 Reasons to Pray in the Holy Spirit

Thus, this is the purpose of this book. To encourage you to war by praying in the Spirit and the many other reasons you should pray using your heavenly language... 14 to be exact... for now -).

Tracy L. Williams

When we receive the gift of salvation and the gift of the Holy Spirit we enter God's world, His atmosphere – a self-less life right here on this earth. His concerns become our concerns. Our pure heart and willingness welcome His Spirit, the Holy Spirit, to take us deeper - where the DEEP calls to the deep (Psalms 42:7). The next chapters will not exhaust this area, but it will increase your faith in this area.

GO AHEAD... ENTER IN.

14 Reasons to Pray in the Holy Spirit

IT'S A NEW LANGUAGE – HEAVEN'S

#1

And they were all filled with the Holy Spirit and began to speak with other tongues, as the Spirit gave them utterance. ~Acts 2:4 NKJV

14 Reasons to Pray in the Holy Spirit

You have a new language, the language of Heaven, empowered and administered by the Holy Spirit. It's a new lifestyle that comes with a new nature received in Jesus Christ. Just as in France they speak French and in Italy they speak Italian, similarly, in the Holy Spirit we speak in tongues - in the spirit.

If any person be in Christ he is a new creature altogether, the old (previous moral and spiritual condition) has passed away (2 Corinthians 5:17). It's up to us to receive and walk in all this "newness".

It is also evident that with our new language comes power – supernatural power – on our natural. The Holy Spirit, Himself, fills us with His presence and speaks through us as we allow Him to.

But you will receive power *and* ability when the Holy Spirit comes upon you; and you will be My witnesses [to tell people about Me] both in Jerusalem and in all Judea, and Samaria, and even to the ends of the earth. Acts 1:8

The Holy Spirit is God in us... therefore God prays through us, for us, by His Spirit.

And they were all filled [that is, diffused throughout their being] with the Holy Spirit and began to speak in other tongues (different languages), as the Spirit was giving them the ability to speak out [clearly and appropriately]. Acts 2:4

Wow... He is amazing. The Holy Spirit is one with God. We are one with God. He's with Him and we are with THEM! Let Him intercede for us. We receive such peace when we allow the Holy Spirit to pray what we may not know to pray. This is God praying through us. When God prays through us He will only pray His word.

The Holy Spirit is the concordance of the Bible. He knows where every scripture is located... He is the word. We must allow God to be God in our lives. When we do we will experience more of Him (more of heaven here on this earth). Anything that does not line up with God's will, He will cause it to line up... if we trust Him, believe all His word, and pray in the Spirit.

One of the greatest reasons we should be spirit-filled is to give the Holy Spirit access to our hearts. With access to our hearts, He will help us to be the witnesses of Jesus here on this earth that we have been assigned and called to be. With the Holy Spirit's power and His voice flowing through us we can not fail.

...how God anointed Jesus of Nazareth with the Holy Spirit and with great power; and He went around doing good and healing all who were oppressed by the devil, because God was with Him. Acts 10:38

We can do nothing without the Holy Spirit (that will give God the glory). Without Him… we are merely natural with no supernatural results.

14 Reasons to Pray in the Holy Spirit

PRAYER IS NOT TO MEN, BUT DIRECTLY TO GOD

#2

    For he who speaks in a tongue does not speak to men but to God, for no one understands him; however, in the sprit he speaks mysteries.
~1 Corinthians 14:2 NKJV

14 Reasons to Pray in the Holy Spirit

One of the key reasons to pray in the Spirit is that the devil cannot understand you, because you speak directly to God. This is one of the greatest weapons included in the full armor of God that the devil would love for the believer to never be acquainted with.

... lest Satan should get an advantage over us. For we are not ignorant of his devices. 2 Corinthians 2:11 KJV

The believer who *is not* ignorant of the devil's device (to keep us without knowledge of what God has provided) becomes an immediate threat to the kingdom of darkness. Specifically, the believer who is allowing this gift to flow through them. The devil is a defeated enemy and doesn't stand a chance against the believer who is equipped with this knowledge and who is applying it. It is sad to say, but he has blinded some with the deception (lie) that the gift of praying in the Spirit is not for all who believe.

...among them the god of this world [Satan] has blinded the minds of the unbelieving to prevent them from seeing the illuminating light of the gospel of the glory of Christ, who is the image of God. 2 Corinthians 4:4

...and that they may come to their senses and escape from the trap of the devil, having been held captive by him to do his will. 2 Timothy 2:26

Prayer is relationship, and prayer is spiritual. What is being spiritual? This means that there are spiritual, demonic forces that are unseen that would attempt to interrupt, hinder, or come against our prayers to God or our intercession as we partner with God in standing in the gap for others.

...Then he said to me, "Do not be afraid, Daniel, for from the first day that you set your heart on understanding this and on humbling yourself before your God, your words were heard, and I have come in response to your words. But the prince of the kingdom of Persia was standing

in opposition to me for twenty-one days. Then, behold, Michael, one of the chief [of the celestial] princes, came to help me, for I had been left there with the kings of Persia. Daniel 10:12-13

When we pray in the Spirit, we pray directly to God unhindered and unchecked by outside forces. The moment we speak God's word angels move to perform His word in the earth.

He dreamed that there was a ladder (stairway) placed on the earth, and the top of it reached [out of sight] toward heaven; and [he saw] the angels of God ascending and descending on it [going to and from heaven]. Genesis 28:12

Prayer in the Spirit gives no room to the devil. The devil cannot understand, comprehend, or interfere with what we release or pray in the Spirit, therefore he cannot assign fallen angels to fight against the victory we have received and declared.

Be refreshed by the Holy Spirit. In moments where you may feel drained, powerless or faithless, pray in the Spirit. People, circumstances, and situations can be used to get you to that place of feeling drained, powerless or faithless, but you don't have to stay there. More than likely you have drifted into "feelings" and need to get back into faith. Pray in the Spirit.

Pray in the Spirit. The Holy Spirit aids and helps us. Instead of trying to figure things out (pulling out scriptures, and creating a confession) God may say, "The valuable time you use to do that, you can use to pray in the Spirit and trust Me - it's already done." By faith, we must believe that He is, and that He is the rewarder of those who diligently seek Him (Hebrews 11:6), and His wisdom.

Let's not try to figure it out ourselves. Just pray in the Spirit. That prayer is perfect prayer. We are called to steward our time wisely. Praying in the spirit is the best way to pray and believe God. We must lose control (surrender our will for His will), and the allow the Holy Spirit to have His way and to perfect those things that concern us. Pray in the Spirit and trust God.

14 Reasons to Pray in the Holy Spirit

I have found myself relaxing from trying to prove to myself how wise I have become in the scripture and what to say and what to pray…. I've humbled myself to trust that the Holy Spirit will hit the bull's eye every time I open my mouth and allow Him to use my vocal cords in His ministry. His ministry is for me and others… all the time. He is never limited to the one praying… I believe that once He gets someone with a willing heart and an open mouth He will release heaven without limits.

Jesus said to them, "My food is to do the will of Him Who sent Me and to completely finish His work. John 4:34

For I have come down from Heaven, not to do My own will, but to do the will of Him Who sent Me. John 6:38

---

14 Reasons to Pray in the Holy Spirit

#3 MYSTERIES OF GOD ARE RELEASED

And He said, "To you it has been given to know the mysteries of the kingdom of God, but to the rest *it is given* in parables, that 'Seeing they may not see, and hearing they may not understand.'" ~Luke 8:10 NKJV

14 Reasons to Pray in the Holy Spirit

As stewards or keepers of the mysteries of God we are assigned by God to manage, maintain, and administer heaven on earth. We speak the mysteries of God when we pray in the Spirit.

For one who speaks in an *unknown* tongue does not speak to people but to God; for no one understands him *or* catches his meaning, but by the Spirit he speaks mysteries [secret truths, hidden things]. I Corinthians 14:2

We have been given stewardship over the mysteries of God. A mystery is anything that has not been revealed to the natural mind. Which means a natural man/woman cannot receive nor understand God and His works. A born again, spirit-filled believer is equipped with the Holy Spirit. God speaks to our spirit and reveals who He is to our spirit. Therefore, when we pray in the Spirit we are speaking God's word, what He has said, and what He has done.

O Lord, how great are Your works! Your thoughts are very deep. A senseless man does not know, nor does a fool understand this. Psalms 92:5, 6 NKJV

In scripture and theology, a steward is a minister of Christ, whose duty is to dispense the provisions of the gospel, to preach its doctrines and administer its ordinances. All of this sounds great and with understanding we will do an excellent work in doing so. However, but if we are not completely sure what God has assigned for us to do or what He would have us to speak or say concerning His mysteries, His plan, His order - what He has already done - we can pray in the spirit and it's a done deal. God seeks out the faithful... those that are found faithful to be stewards of His mysteries... those who pray faithfully in the Holy Spirit.

"...but we speak God's wisdom in a mystery, the *wisdom* once hidden [from man, but now revealed to us by God, that wisdom] which God predestined before the ages to our glory [to lift us into the glory of His presence]." 1 Corinthians 2:7

14 Reasons to Pray in the Holy Spirit

I am encouraging you to pray in the Spirit. If you pray in the Spirit you, will eliminate attacks of sickness. The Holy Spirit can and will war on your behalf. He knows what the enemy will try to bring your way. What if you don't have time or if you don't remember to declare Proverbs 3 over your divine health? I guarantee you the Holy Spirit will remember, because He only prays God's word.

Do not be wise in your own eyes: fear the Lord [with reverent awe and obedience] and turn [entirely] away from evil. It will be health to your body [your marrow, your nerves, your sinews, your muscles—all your inner parts] and refreshment (physical well-being) to your bones. Proverbs 3:7,8

Let a man so consider us, as servants of Christ and stewards of the mysteries of God.
I Corinthians 4:1 NKJV

---

14 Reasons to Pray in the Holy Spirit

#4   THE WONDERFUL WORKS OF GOD ARE DECLARED

Cretans and Arabs – we hear them speaking in our own tongues the wonderful works of God.
~Acts 2:11 NKJV

14 Reasons to Pray in the Holy Spirit

When we speak in the Spirit, the wonderful works of God are being released. Just like when God spoke, "Let there be light." We speak God's word and His heart through our mouths – we yield our vocal cords to His ministry. The ministry of the Holy Spirit here on the earth is spiritual and we must understand that when we operate out of a spiritual understanding of who we are we can be used of Him greatly.

Now, picture this...God speaks to Jesus - Jesus speaks to the Holy Spirit - the Holy Spirit speaks to us. What was said from God comes through our mouths. God is in heaven, Jesus is seated at His right side, and the Holy Spirit is both there and in us. We are His representatives here on the earth...representatives filled with the Holy Spirit. Remember, God has placed His word in our mouths (Isa 51:16) that we may plant the new heaven and the new earth.

And He raised us up together with Him [when we believed], and seated us with Him in the

**heavenly places, [because we are] in Christ Jesus...
Ephesians 2:6**

How great are Your works, O God! Why not more of God? It's time for us to experience more of God. If we keep experiencing more of us and not more of God it will cause us to experience more of this world and its defeat, frustrations, and failure. On the other hand, if instead we're experiencing more of God we will experience more of His kingdom and its benefits positioned right here on the earth for us to enjoy and help others to experience the same. I want more of God. You should want more of God.

We should want to live a spiritual life and not a carnal life. If someone is calling you "too spiritual" be mindful – that is the place to be in this hour. Pray in the Spirit more! Don't allow the devil to back you down from praying in the Spirit more. This is the answer. This is the key. This is the missing ingredient. This is where the power is. This is where the victory is.

14 Reasons to Pray in the Holy Spirit

Let's take a quick intermission... yes, in a book. I have a quick insert to share with you before moving to the next chapter - 😉.

I was on a flight to Seattle while working on this chapter, and I looked out the window and saw clouds and mountains. As I listened to the teaching I'd previously taught in this area and transcribed what the Lord would have me to take from it my heart was encouraged to hear this teaching all over again.

<u>The devil is real</u>. Our war is not with people. We have a good fight of faith and we already win. We will experience more of that victory if we pray in the Spirit. This doesn't mean the fights and the wars will not come it just means the more we are prayed up, and girded up in prayer, and built up in our most holy faith - we will stand. And, when we have done all to stand we will keep on standing.

We need to choose to spend more time in God's word and turn off somethings that have literally been put in place to distract us from this awesome spiritual life. At times our thoughts will make us think we are missing out on things, even missing out on life. <u>Our life is Christ</u>. This new life here on the earth is only a glimpse of the real life we will soon experience at the coming our King Jesus.

It never fails, the moment you make up your mind to meditate or study God's word a "sleepy spirit" tries to come on you. We cannot be ignorant of Satan's devices (2 Corinthians 2:11). Just rebuke that "sleepy spirit" and keep studying God's word. Wake up earlier. Stay up later. Whatever we need to do - it's up to us to experience the great and mighty works of God, most importantly His presence and His love.

God wants us to wake up to Him. We do not know the time or the hour that Jesus will gather us to Himself. He is coming back for the Church. We want to ensure the seal of the Holy Spirit is on us. We should be about our Father's business and be a Church without spot, wrinkle, or blemish. This will take continued cultivating of obedient acts. Look for opportunities to obey and it will soon become natural… not hard nor burdensome.

But the word *is* very near you, in your mouth and in your heart, that you may do it. Deuteronomy 30:14 NKJV

Prayer in the Spirit will keep us sensitive to the voice of God and grace us with the ability to obey His voice. We do not want to be caught like the foolish virgins who had no oil when the Bridegroom came (Matthew 25). We want to be prepared at His coming. We do not want to be caught just doing our own thing. We should be excited about God's word. Why not be prepared?

Prayer in the Spirit helps and equips us to obey the ministry of the Holy Spirit.

14 Reasons to Pray in the Holy Spirit

The Holy Spirit has a ministry on this earth. It is revealed to those who have the habit of obeying and being led by the Spirit of God - not by the dictates of their flesh.

I Corinthians 2: 10-16

End of intermission. Let's get to the next inspiring chapter of "14 Reasons to Pray in the Holy Spirit"!

Tracy L. Williams

14 Reasons to Pray in the Holy Spirit

GOD IS MAGNIFIED/GLORIFIED

#5

For they heard them speak with tongues and magnify God. Then Peter answered, "Can anyone forbid water, that these should not be baptized who have received the Holy Spirit just as we have." ~Acts 10:46, 47 NKJV

14 Reasons to Pray in the Holy Spirit

We are God's mouth piece here on this earth. We can't get caught up on sleep and what we see tangibly on the surface or what's right in front of us. There is communication going on in Heaven: (For I neither received it *(this revelation)* from man, nor was I taught it, but it came through the revelation of Jesus Christ. Galatians 1:12 NKJV) **Italics my words.*

- God speaks to the Son (our Lord, our Savior, our brother Jesus).
- The Son speaks those words from God directly to the Holy Spirit.
- The Holy Spirit, Who lives in and through us, speaks directly what He heard from the Son (Jesus) to us.
- We are supposed to speak what came from the Holy Spirit, through the Son, by God here on this earth!

This in turn causes (manifests) heaven to be released in the earth… thus heaven on earth. Not just cliché' but truth - God the Father, Jesus the Son, the Holy Spirit, and us. They are one, and we are one with them. The Holy Spirit is the representative of the Godhead here on the earth. We are a dwelling place, an extension of the Spirit of God. God receives the glory, Jesus is gloried, and Christ (the Anointing, the Holy Spirit) is magnified through us.

"And I have put My words in your mouth and have covered you with the shadow of My hand, that I may fix the (new) heavens as a tabernacle and lay the foundations of a (new) earth and say to Zion, you are My people." Isaiah 51:16

The Holy Spirit is the seal of our redemption. He is the precious promise given to us by God. When we pray in the Spirit we are praying in His language. If we remain at a place where we are allowing the Holy Spirit to pray through us we are assuring ourselves that He is with us - coupled with a right heart and blameless (without sin). It is important that we be reminded that Jesus knew no sin and that He became sin for us so that we would be free and no longer acquainted with sin. Anyone practicing sin should repent, change for good, and receive a fresh anointing from God (2 Cor. 5:21). We don't want to be caught in any hour without the prominent seal of the Holy Spirit. When the Lord returns for the church this is the seal He will recognize and be acquainted with.

Prayer that you can make personal:
In Jesus name Father, "Create in me a clean heart, O God, and renew a right, persevering, and steadfast spirit within me. Cast me not away from Your presence and take not Your Holy Spirit from me. Restore to me the joy of Your salvation and uphold me with a willing spirit." Psalms 51:10-12

There is another seal that we should not be found with or acquainted with and that's the seal of the beast. Check out the following scripture:

And then I saw thrones and sitting on them were those to whom judgment [that is, the authority to act as judges] was given. And I saw the souls of those who had been beheaded because of their testimony of Jesus and because of the word of God, and those who had refused to worship the

beast or his image and had not accepted his mark on their forehead and on their hand; and they came to life and reigned with Christ for a thousand years. Revelation 20:4

When praying in the Spirit we are reminded that we have peace with God and have entered His rest. Peace is still in this place, in this realm, in this dimension – even while in your prayer closet you know you have entered the heavenlies while still in the body.

---

14 Reasons to Pray in the Holy Spirit

IT'S YOUR SPIRIT PRAYING

#6

For if I pray in a tongue, my spirit prays, but my understanding is unfruitful. ~1 Corinthians 14:14 NKJV

14 Reasons to Pray in the Holy Spirit

This is not your natural man praying. This is not the flesh praying. It's your spirit-man praying. For us to be more spiritual, we must allow our spirit to pray through us. We must pray with understanding, not religiously. Not mocking the sound (as we have heard from others who pray in the Spirit), but truly yielding your vocal cords and allowing the Holy Spirit to have His way through your voice... through your mouth.

The Spirit of God, the Holy Spirit, has His own language. I believe how we speak when we are spirit-filled - with evidence of speaking in another tongue - is the language of Heaven. When we pray in the Spirit, we are speaking in the Spirit. It's God, Himself speaking through us. Powerful, effective, awesome... period.

We have been created in the image and in the likeness of God. We are just like God. God is our Father and we look like Him. We are a spirit – God is a Spirit (John 4:24). We have a soul and we live in a body (I Thessalonians 5:23). It is not vice versa as we've heard in the world – body and soul – leaving the spirit completely out. Once we became born again we were to instantly act like God. Prayer in the Spirit causes us to talk like God. When we pray in the Spirit, it's the Holy Spirit, Who is the representative of the Godhead here on the earth, speaking the perfect will of God through us.

Then God said, "Let Us make man in Our image, according to Our likeness; let them have dominion..." Genesis 1:26a NKJV

The initial scripture (mentioned at the beginning of this chapter – I Corinthians 14:14) shares that we will not understand what we are saying but, that should not stop us from knowing by faith that we are releasing the perfect will of God through our mouths. Everything God has done is already done. As we pray in the Spirit we are used by God to release heaven on earth.

'Your kingdom come, Your will be done on earth as it is in heaven." Matthew 6:10

14 Reasons to Pray in the Holy Spirit

God reveals His will, His plan, His agenda, His order, His word to our spirit - not our flesh. As we pray more in the Spirit we will operate out of the ability to discern when to share what God has placed on our hearts and when not to. What is shared in this book is spiritually discerned. A natural man, or even a born-again man who is still carnal, will not be able to comprehend going to the next level in the Spirit. The word of God shares that we should be teachers and not babies any longer (still needing milk) in living out the full counsel of God's word (Hebrews 5:13). Instead we should be spiritually mature, able to eat the meat of God's word...receive revelation and understanding that is not revealed to our natural man – to our senses. Praying in the Spirit is meat.

But God has revealed them to us through His Spirit. For the Spirit searches all things, yes, the deep things of God. For what man knows the things of a man except the spirit of the man which is in him? Even so no one knows the things of God except the Spirit of God. Now we have received, not the spirit of the world, but the Spirit who is

from God, that we might know the things that have been freely given to us by God.
I Corinthians 2:10-12 NKJV

Praying in the Spirit will remind you of God's peace that surpasses the natural mind, the natural understanding. The longer you pray and yield you will experience a calm state – a sense of knowing that all is well. God's peace is perfect. Experience more of it by praying in the Spirit.

Psalm 46:10 ~ Isaiah 26:3

14 Reasons to Pray in the Holy Spirit

THE FIRE OF GOD IS RELEASED

#7

    Then there appeared to them divided tongues, as of fire, and one sat upon each of them. ~Acts 2:3 NKJV

14 Reasons to Pray in the Holy Spirit

Praying in the Spirit comes from heaven. Once again, it's the language of heaven. When we pray in the Spirit it releases the fire of God. Without understanding, it will be done traditionally or religiously.

Praying corporately on one accord in a ministry setting helps to cultivate your prayer life. If you are not praying in the Spirit at church or in a church setting where the anointing is present and there are other believers of like precious faith praying in the Spirit (basically a spiritual atmosphere where the gifts of the Spirit are being stirred up and cultivated) more than likely you are not praying in the spirit the way you should at home. Don't be deceived - this can be a great way to evaluate yourself.

Examine yourselves as to whether you are in the faith. Test yourselves. Do you not know yourselves, that Jesus Christ is in you?—unless indeed you are disqualified.
2 Corinthians 13:5 NKJV

Corporate prayer or corporate intercession is on purpose. Not only is it a set time to war spiritually - before a set service, calling things to divine order; interceding on behalf of others; or calling in the harvest - but it causes unity and one accord. When we pray in the spirit we put out natural fires - anything that is not like God that has stirred up confusion, strife, contention, or darkness can be put out spiritually by praying in agreement and declaring the victory. When we pray in the Spirit corporately, on purpose, we prepare the way for the harvest God sends to the house of the Lord. We cause Revelations 11:15 to come alive that states:

... "The kingdoms of this world have become the kingdoms of our Lord and of His Christ, and He shall reign forever and ever!" Revelations 11:15 NKJV

This atmosphere ushers in the fire of God's glory that will cancel or destroy any manifestation of the devil and ensure that only the Kingdom of God will be demonstrated and experienced – love, joy, peace, righteousness, and the Holy Spirit. Those who are wise will see this revelation, understand, and put action to what they believe without a hint of fear.

"No weapon that is formed against you will succeed; and every tongue that rises against you in judgment you will condemn. This [peace, righteousness, security, and triumph over opposition] is the heritage of the servants of the LORD, and this is their vindication from Me," says the LORD. Isaiah 54:17

The fire of God that comes with prayer in the Spirit will even deal with the person praying (as an act of purification that the one praying will remain pure and undefiled in His presence). This makes room for greater use of that person by the Holy Spirit and His ministry.

Therefore, if anyone cleanses himself from the latter, he will be a vessel for honor, sanctified and useful for the Master, prepared for every good work. 2 Timothy 2:21 NKJV

Tracy L. Williams

When we pray in the Spirit we come from religion and tradition to relationship.

---

14 Reasons to Pray in the Holy Spirit

#8 IT'S EVIDENCE OF THE SPIRIT-FILLED LIFE

And these signs will follow those who believe: in My name they will cast out demons; they will speak with new tongues; they will take up serpents; and if they drink anything deadly, it will by no means hurt them; they will lay hands on the sick, and they will recover. ~Mark 16:17-18 NKJV

14 Reasons to Pray in the Holy Spirit

People need to see that we, as believers, are spirit-filled, and that Christ is in us and operating through us. Our family members, co-workers, and friends all need this evidence/witness to know God as we do… that He is real, and that He has changed us from the inside out. Our actions will always speak louder than our words. In the New Testament, in the book of Matthew we begin to hear a lot about the religious acts of the scribes and the Pharisees, and the characteristic that stands out the most is hypocrisy. Hypocrites tell others to do what they are not doing themselves.

"Woe to you, [self-righteous] scribes and Pharisees, hypocrites! For you clean the outside of the cup and of the plate, but inside they are full of extortion *and* robbery and self-indulgence (unrestrained greed). You [spiritually] blind Pharisee, first clean the inside of the cup and of the plate [examine and change your inner self to conform to God's precepts], so that the outside [your public life and deeds] may be clean also. Matthew 23:25, 26

Some people have shared with me when I'm out soul winning that this is one reason that they do not want anything to do with God or going to church. They've been around others – specifically family – who, after attending church, return home and live and speak contrary to the word they've received. Prayer in the Spirit can help us mature spiritually and give us access to the fruit of the Spirit to being made known through our actions and how we live our lives.

Therefore, by their fruits you will know them. Not everyone who says to Me, 'Lord, Lord,' shall enter the kingdom of Heaven, but he who does the will of My Father in heaven. Matthew 7:20, 21 NKJV

When we pray in the spirit we become spiritually alert to spiritual things, which is so key to being a king and a priest in the Kingdom of God. Examples of spiritual things can include evil spirits, principalities, powers of darkness, and spiritual hosts of wickedness in heavenly places and here on the earth.

14 Reasons to Pray in the Holy Spirit

Once we get born again it can seem like all hell breaks loose and everything and everyone is coming against us. That's not entirely true - it only seems that way. Those things were already taking place before we received new life in Christ. The difference is we were not spiritually alert to recognize it wasn't only natural wars happening in our lives but spiritual wars as well. We cannot handle what this world or the god of this world presents to detour us from faith if we are not spirit-filled with the power of God, standing by the grace of God, and continuing to stand when we have done all to stand.

...among them the god of this world [Satan] has blinded the minds of the unbelieving to prevent them from seeing the illuminating light of the gospel of the glory of Christ, who is the image of God. 2 Corinthians 4:4

Praying in the spirit gives us backbone. When everyone else is complaining about the changes in the office - the downsizing or the pay cuts - the spiritually strong believer is rejoicing, remaining joyful, without despair, basically a beacon of light. This is evidence that there is something greater in us operating through us. The supernatural on our natural man is an invisible strength that causes others to want to know what keeps us going, what makes us so strong, what keeps us positive, and what gives us hope even in the midst.

Evidence of a spirit-filled life is the continued choice of life in every decision. You can almost, always discern how spiritual someone is as a result of the choices they make. Prayer in the spirit builds us up to remain spirit-led, hearing God's voice, sensitive to the atmosphere (whether it needs a shifting or not), discerning of spirits, and gives us wisdom to speak what we hear in our hearts and bring change. Praying in the Spirit enables the ability to discern between good and evil, right and wrong. In this hour, and every hour while the earth remains, we need to know who's for us and who's not - all the while remaining in love. It's only by the power of the Holy Spirit and His full operation in and through us that we can be successful – fruitful.

14 Reasons to Pray in the Holy Spirit

Then you shall again discern between the righteous and the wicked, between one who serves God and one who does not serve Him. ~Malachi 3:18 NKJV

But the natural man does not receive the things of the Spirit of God, for they are foolishness to him; nor can he know *them,* because they are spiritually discerned. ~1 Corinthians 2:14 NKJV

But solid food belongs to those who are of full age, *that is,* those who by reason of use have their senses exercised to discern both good and evil. ~Hebrews 5:14 NKJV

---

14 Reasons to Pray in the Holy Spirit

IT'S A SIGN FOR NON-BELIEVERS

#9

Therefore, tongues are for a sign, not to those who believe but to unbelievers; but prophesying is not for unbelievers but for those who believe. ~I Corinthians 14:22 NKJV

14 Reasons to Pray in the Holy Spirit

There is no peace for the wicked. Once unbelievers recognize the place of peace operating and evident in the believer's life they want to know more. God's rest is found in this place of yielding to the ministry of the Holy Spirit. It's a place of losing control and surrendering your will to the will of God - understanding that God will not make us do anything and that He will allow whatever we allow. Prayer in the Spirit allows God to speak His agenda, His order, His will through us and for us into existence. When God is receiving the glory for our lives non-believers desire to know the God we serve.

When you pray in the spirit it is absolute perfect prayer. It's the Holy Spirit praying – speaking through you making those things perfect that concerns you. The most common answer I receive when out in the mission field (right in our communities) regarding why people have not received Jesus as their Lord and Savior or why they do not attend a local church is because they have relatives or people around them that speak Jesus, and how good He is, but their lives and lifestyles are completely contrary. They can not see the difference between the born again, church going believer and themselves. So, they choose to remain in the world as non-believers.

The world must see how good God is and that He is a restoring God who's real. The world does not need to see the Church (us) worried and concerned and always going through but never seeing the victory promised.

"The LORD will perfect that which concerns me; Your mercy, O LORD, endures forever; do not forsake the works of Your hands." Psalms 138:8 NKJV

What are somethings that could cause us to be concerned? Finances, family, relationships, health issues, not enough, too much, somebody's upset with us, people that don't understand, oppression, depression, fear, and finally... death. The word of God shares that God already knows what we have need of before we ask (Matthew 6:32), so He prefers that we not worry about anything or anyone. He's got us. That is why He sent the Holy Spirit. Therefore, Jesus prayed forth the Holy Spirit. And this is why the Holy Spirit came - to help us.

So too the [Holy] Spirit comes to our aid and bears us up in our weakness; for we do not know what prayer to offer nor how to offer it worthily as we ought, but the Spirit Himself goes to meet our supplication and pleads in our behalf with unspeakable yearnings and groanings too deep for utterance. Romans 8:26

The Holy Spirit helps us in prayer by dealing directly with whatever may be on our hearts by putting God's word on it. He is the Holly Spirit... He is God and He will only speak God's word. Sure, we could go to the index or glossary of the Bible and look up the scriptures that deal directly with a specific area of challenge or that will increase our faith in that area but, the Holy Spirit is the living word and He can help in eradicating situations or tests of faith immediately. The choice is yours... either your desire to do it yourself or your complete trust in God and His supernatural ability in you.

All the Holy Spirit needs is for us to yield our vocal cords and He will pray on our behalf if we will only believe. This is by far the greatest benefit of our salvation... literally having God, Himself manifested through us by way of His Spirit.

Take a moment to consider our Lord and our Savior, Jesus. When He graced this earth with His presence He was not walking around with a Bible. He was (and is) the Word. He was spirit-filled (Luke 3:22). And He had immediate access to the wisdom of God as He walked with the anointing, Christ (not His last name) He had immediate access to the wisdom of God. Jesus is our great example.

But first and most importantly seek (aim at, strive after) His kingdom and His righteousness [His way of doing and being right—the attitude and character of God], and all these things will be given to you also. Matthew 6:33

I truly believe Jesus prayed and spoke in His prayer language (in tongues) as well. I believe this is the language of Heaven and we have been graced with the ability to do so here on the earth. The Holy Spirit filled the body of Jesus and He was empowered, just like we are when the Holy Spirit fills us with His baptism.

For indeed I did not receive it from man, nor was I taught it, but I received it through a [direct] revelation of Jesus Christ. Galatians 1:12

And there are also many other things which Jesus did, which if they were recorded one by one, I suppose that even the world itself could not contain the books that would be written. John 21:25

It's up to us what we will believe concerning the Holy Spirit and His baptism. I believe the more we believe the greater the power will flow through us – we become bolder and more confident. And if we only believe to yet another level, we will see great manifestations (tangible answers) of things thought of or considered but never actually prayed out or even asked of God.

Tracy L. Williams

> Now to Him who is able to [carry out His purpose and] do superabundantly more than all that we dare ask or think [infinitely beyond our greatest prayers, hopes, or dreams], according to His power that is at work within us, to Him be the glory in the church and in Christ Jesus throughout all generations forever and ever. Amen.
> ~Ephesians 3:20, 21

14 Reasons to Pray in the Holy Spirit

Peace I leave with you; My [own] peace I now give *and* bequeath to you. Not as the world gives do I give to you. Do not let your hearts be troubled, neither let them be afraid. [Stop allowing yourselves to be agitated and disturbed; and do not permit yourselves to be fearful and intimidated and cowardly and unsettled.] ~John 14:27 AMPC

Tracy L. Williams

14 Reasons to Pray in the Holy Spirit

IT'S SELFLESS INTERCESSION

#10

...praying always with all prayer and supplication in the Spirit, being watchful to this end with all perseverance and supplication for all the saints... ~Eph 6:18 NKJV

14 Reasons to Pray in the Holy Spirit

I personally recall waking up earlier than usual in the morning (wide awake, not sleepy, even with only a few hours of sleep) and having a sense of urgency to pray in the spirit. At times, while praying, I would have visions at times while praying of people being delivered, fights ceasing, children set free, and evil acts exposed. I may not know exactly who I was praying for or what country they were residents of, but out of obedience and my belief I knew I was interceding effectively for others. When we pray in the Spirit as the Lord leads, at times we could be praying for the Church (the Body of Christ). Intercession is necessary. We could be used to persevere in prayer for someone else. Therefore, it's selfless - no longer prayer time for what we may think we need, but consecrated prayer time to meet the need of another.

He saw that there was no man, and wondered that there was no intercessor; therefore His own arm brought salvation for Him; and His own righteousness, it sustained Him. Isaiah 59:16 NKJV

Tracy L. Williams

God seeks prayer warriors who are confident that their every need has been met and that they are already covered in prayer by the Chief Intercessor - the Holy Spirit – to use their prayer time to intercede and stand in the gap for other people. This type of intercessor will be used to intercede for natural bloodlines and nations. It's selfless prayer and deems great rewards. I believe our early morning prayer time should be more concentrated on warring against principalities and powers, in addition to interceding for our loved ones, and praying in the Spirit. As we pray in the Spirit, we are covering nations (other peoples' loved ones – unknowingly) yet yielding to allow the Holy Spirit to have His way while praying through us.

Likewise, the Spirit also helps in our weaknesses. For we do not know what we should pray for as we ought, but the Spirit Himself makes intercession for us with groanings which cannot be uttered. Romans 8:26 NKJV

God's heart is that not one perish, that not one experience eternal misery and end up in the wrong place. The word shares in 1 Timothy 2:1-4 NKJV, Therefore I exhort first of all that supplications, prayers, intercessions, *and* giving of thanks be made for all men, for kings and all who are in authority, that we may lead a quiet and peaceable life in all godliness and reverence. For this *is* good and acceptable in the sight of God our Savior, who desires all men to be saved and to come to the knowledge of the truth.

Even during our time of consecrated prayer in the Spirit we could be praying for all that are in authority….as admonished in God's word. The only way we can pray for people we do not know or intercede for effectively is in the Spirit. The Holy Spirit knows what they need; may it be answers, resources, protection, wisdom, love, healing, restoration, relationships mended, etc. Only He, the Holy Spirit, can be in multiple locations at one time through our vocal cords. When we yield our vocal cords to His ministry He will cover areas of God's heart…. God's heart is people and the salvation of souls. Can He count on you? Even Jesus prayed for those who persecuted Him - surely it should be even easier for us to pray for those we may not know.

For the Lord's portion is His people; Deuteronomy 32:9a

When we rise early and allow the Holy Spirit to pray through us in intercession these are the deep things of God. Our spirit-man never sleeps and neither does the Holy Spirit. Many times, we have to rebuke our flesh and allow this divine interaction to take place. Our spirit and the Spirit of God are one. With them working together souls will be saved in our families, in our nations, in the world. This is God's heart. This is the bigger plan and the greater works that we have been called to accomplish by grace and the power of God.

I assure you, most solemnly I tell you, if anyone steadfastly believes in Me, he will himself be able to do the things that I do; and he will do even greater things than these, because I go to the Father. John 14:12 AMPC

14 Reasons to Pray in the Holy Spirit

The Holy Spirit will remind us to do and to say God's will and God's Word. He causes us to remember things.

"The memory of the righteous is blessed (Proverbs 10:7) NKJV."

Tracy L. Williams

14 Reasons to Pray in the Holy Spirit

#11   **THE ONE PRAYING IS REMINDED OF WHAT GOD SAID**

But the Helper, the Holy Spirit, whom the Father will send in My name, He will teach you all things, and bring to your remembrance all things I said to you. ~John 14:26 NKJV

Specific things the Lord has spoken to us will come back to our memory as we pray in the Spirit, as well as when we meditate on God's word... whether it be a specific scripture that will now become alive to us or direction or the next step to take in pursuing vision or a goal given by God. Prayer in the Spirit fills our mouth with God's word <u>only</u> and releases His word <u>only</u>. We cannot miss praying the perfect will of God when we pray in the Spirit.

**Who satisfies your mouth with good things, so that your youth is renewed like the eagle's.
Psalm 103:5 NKJV**

Desires that are given by God can only lie dormant for a time. When God has spoken something to us or has given us instruction we will not be able to forget it until it is completed. No matter how much we put other things before it or put in on the back burner, as we pray in the Spirit, it will come to our memory. Prayer in the Spirit is a beautiful 'nudge' by the Holy Spirit, Himself... by God, Himself to remind us of what is important, what is crucial at times.

The Holy Spirit will also remind us when we are not in the will of God or doing what God's word has commanded. This comes to us in the way of conviction. Conviction by the Holy Spirit is good and causes us to change for the better. He doesn't point out our wrong, but He helps us by sharing with us inwardly that we have gone in the wrong way – that we have gone in error - and He leads us back to the way of truth when we allow Him to.

He is the Spirit of truth, and when the Spirit of truth prays through us, more than likely we will be compelled to confront or deal with any areas that are not aligned with God and His ways if we desire the presence of the Holy Spirit to remain. The ministry of the Holy Spirit as mentioned earlier is here on this earth – operating through the born-again believer who believes. He will gently prune those who possess His presence while at the same time bring judgment to the world in preparation for our soon coming King.

...the Spirit of truth, whom the world cannot receive, because it neither sees Him nor knows

Him; but you know Him, for He dwells with you and will be in you. John 14:17 NKJV

Tracy L. Williams

The Wok of the Holy Spirit

John 16:7-11 NKJV

Nevertheless, I tell you the truth. It is to your advantage that I go away; for if I do not go away, the Helper will not come to you; but if I depart, I will send Him to you. And when He has come, He will convict the world of sin, and of righteousness, and of judgment: of sin, because they do not believe in Me; of righteousness, because I go to My Father and you see Me no more; of judgment, because the ruler of this world is judged.

14 Reasons to Pray in the Holy Spirit

#12   THE ONE PRAYING IS PERSONALLY EDIFIED

He who speaks in a tongue edifies himself, but he who prophesies edifies the church.
~1 Corinthians 14:4 NKJV

14 Reasons to Pray in the Holy Spirit

An edifice is a building; a structure; a fabric; but appropriately, a large or splendid building. The word is not applied to a mean (average) building, but to temples, churches or elegant mansion-houses, and to other great structures.

We are the Church of the living God and we must edify ourselves daily (first thing in the morning is best 😊). If we choose to go day by day seeking or looking for someone to encourage us, we may not ever be encouraged. This will cause our witness of Jesus to be dull and uninviting. God has placed in us His Spirit - the Holy Spirit. The Holy Spirit is here to help us remain encouraged and to stay in faith. Scripture admonishes us not to allow our hearts to be troubled (John 14:1), and we have a major part in our joy remaining.

If there is ever a moment that I have allowed myself to get down or un-inspired I instantly recognize the enemy's attempt of 'joy removal and peace interruption' and I begin to pray in the Spirit immediately. The moment I pray in the spirit (yield my vocal cords to allow the Holy Spirit to pray through me) I'm refreshed in the presence of the Lord. This is sweet communion with the Holy Spirit - not just communication at a set time daily but an ongoing relationship that opens the door for the Holy Spirit to lead and direct me all day long. Prayer in the Spirit will keep you edified and equip you to edify others.

Edification is encouragement. If we wait for others to encourage us (as mentioned) we may be waiting awhile. So many are about themselves only and never have a thought of being thankful or appreciative enough of others to compliment them or encourage them with words of life. This is where our trust and our confidence in God comes in. God, by His Spirit will encourage us daily if we yield our vocal cords and allow the Holy Spirit to speak life through us and to us. Then when you experience moments where you could become discouraged or moved by the actions of others you will be so built up spiritually that you will not be moved.

14 Reasons to Pray in the Holy Spirit

We become less selfish the more we pray in the Spirit. This positions us so God can use us to edify the Church - our brothers and sisters in the faith.

When we pray in the Spirit we can enter the prophetic realm - a realm where we are empowered to prophesy (to edify, comfort, and exhort) - with the Word of God that comes to our hearts - by the Holy Spirit.

Tracy L. Williams

14 Reasons to Pray in the Holy Spirit

#13   THE ONE PRAYING RECEIVES MOST HOLY FAITH

But you, beloved, build yourselves up (founded) on your most holy faith (make progress, rise like an edifice higher and higher), praying in the Holy Spirit. ~Jude 1:20 AMPC

14 Reasons to Pray in the Holy Spirit

It takes faith to pray in the Spirit and whenever we are in faith God is with us. Prayer in the Spirit causes us to have that God kind of faith that empowers us to speak to mountains, things, and situations and have them removed or replaced. We have what we say when we pray in the Spirit understanding that it is the wisdom of God and the word of God spoken through us.

"Therefore, I say to you, <u>whatever things you ask when you pray</u>, believe that you receive them, and you will have them." Mark 11:24 NKJV

Personally, when I pray in the Spirit 'seated in heavenly places (as shared in Ephesians 2:6) becomes a reality for me. Colossians chapter 3 shares that we have been raised with Christ to a new life and encourages us to seek those things that are above not beneath - to seek heavenly things and not natural carnal things. Heavenly things would be anything lined up with the word of God that will keep our focus on Him and His promises instead of what we may see in the natural that would attempt to cause discouragement or a decrease in faith.

The moment I pray in the Spirit I know I'm going higher and higher (mentally) in the spiritual realm even while still in my body. It's not a spooky nor a scary moment, but a lifestyle of recognizing that my true citizenship is in Heaven even while I live in the earth. Prayer in the Spirit is an immediate connection with God. And I know it's because I pray in faith (I believe that the Holy Spirit is praying and interceding through me) - which literally means God, Himself, is praying through me.

When I pray in the Spirit I give God access to the earth that was given to the devil because of the disobedience of man – Adam (Romans 5:19). Powerful and true. My complete surrender and obedience to yield my vocal cords to the ministry of the Holy Spirit allows God to move in the earth by His word. It's His word that is established here on the earth.

14 Reasons to Pray in the Holy Spirit

Prayer in the Spirit causes us to enter the mind of God. Wow - we can download His thoughts! I constantly write down things (thoughts, inspiration... His word) during prayer, I clearly understand that it's literally God revealing to me His plan and His creations - 'already created'- that just requires a son of God with an open ear, a willing heart, and His desires to birth it here on the earth.

As we build ourselves up in our most holy faith by praying in the Spirit we constantly refresh or reinforce the seal of the Holy Spirit - securing our place in Him.

In Him you also trusted, after you heard the word of truth, the gospel of your salvation; in whom also, having believed, you were sealed with the Holy Spirit of promise, Eph. 1:13 NKJV

We should never allow the seal of the Holy Spirit to loosen and begin to come up like tape can bubble if you do not place pressure on it. We must press to pray in the Spirit. We never want to be found without His adhesive power operating through us and in us. Prayer in the Spirit helps to purify our hearts – the actual residence of the Holy Spirit.

And do not grieve the Holy Spirit of God, by whom you were sealed for the day of redemption. Ephesians 4:30 NKJV

Once again, we are reminded of who we are, and prayer in the Spirit should be our primary language no matter what country we are from.

It's the language of Heaven.
It's eternal.

---

14 Reasons to Pray in the Holy Spirit

TO BE PERFECTED IN LOVE
#14

Such hope (in God's promises) never disappoints us, because God's love has been abundantly poured out within our hearts through the Holy Spirit who was given to us. ~Romans 5:5

14 Reasons to Pray in the Holy Spirit

Because the love of God has been poured into our hearts by the Holy Spirit, it would be wise for us to allow the Holy Spirit complete and total access to our hearts. He is gentle (described as a dove). It's very true to state that we will not be able to walk in the God kind of love without the Holy Spirit. We can say we have Him but, not allowing all that He is to flow through us will hinder the fulfillment we can experience with His full manifestation in our lives. <u>He has been sent to help us love</u>. Having a disagreement or a challenge? Pray in the spirit. Answers and direction will come that will keep you in the love of God which will overcome all evil.

I have loved you just as the Father has loved Me; remain in My love [and do not doubt My love for you]. If you keep My commandments *and* obey My teaching, you will remain in My love, just as I have kept My Father's commandments and remain in His love. I have told you these things so that My joy and delight may be in you, and that your joy may be made full and complete and overflowing. John 15:9-11

The Kingdom of God is of righteousness, love, joy, and peace **IN** the Holy Spirit (Romans 14:17). It's all **IN** the Holy Spirit. We can do nothing (that glorifies Jesus) without the full operation of the Holy Spirit. Love fulfills the law and all its written commands. These laws could not be kept in times past, or in the present, without the supernatural power of God – without His grace, and Christ (the Holy Spirit), the anointing helping us. We have been graced to obey and love is the primary commandment that will keep us experiencing the blessing with an expectation of eternal life.

...keep yourselves in the love of God, looking for the mercy of our Lord Jesus Christ unto eternal life. Jude 21 NKJV

We have received the grace of God to operate in His supernatural abilities. It's supernatural to love your enemies. It's supernatural to walk free from the dominion of sin. It's supernatural to recognize that there is a power working in you to walk in the authority and dominion given by God to be just like Jesus here on the earth. The Holy Spirit helps us to be just like Jesus here on this earth. As we pray in the Spirit we are reminded of who we are and the finished works of Jesus. If we stop trying so hard not to sin and focus on the greatest commandment of all - to love - we will fulfill the law; not be condemned in our thinking, obey God naturally; and keep a focus of love. Once again, without love, (without God Who is Love) we are nothing. The love of God has been poured into our hearts by the entrance of the Holy Spirit. Why not allow Him to speak through us, move through us, pray through us, perfect us and, love through us?

Only stubbornness, intellect, old thinking, tradition, and religion will hinder us from walking in this revelation. The word of God shares in 1 Corinthians 13:1, 8 NKJV, "Though I speak with the tongues of men and of angels, but have not love, I have become sounding brass or a clanging cymbal. Love never fails. But whether there are prophecies, they will fail; whether there are tongues, they will cease; whether there is knowledge, it will vanish away."

Tracy L. Williams

No one has seen God at any time. But if we love one another [with unselfish concern], God abides in us, and His love [the love that is His essence abides in us and] is completed and perfected in us.

In this [union and fellowship with Him], love is completed and perfected with us, so that we may have confidence in the day of judgment [with assurance and boldness to face Him]; because as He is, so are we in this world.

There is no fear in love [dread does not exist]. But perfect (complete, full-grown) love drives out fear, because fear involves [the expectation of divine] punishment, so the one who is afraid [of God's judgment] is not perfected in love [has not grown into a sufficient understanding of God's love].
~John 4:12, 17, 18

14 Reasons to Pray in the Holy Spirit

CONCLUSION:
SPIRITUAL WARFARE IS REAL

'to the intent that now the manifold wisdom of God might be made known by the church to the principalities and powers in the heavenly *places,* according to the eternal purpose which He accomplished in Christ Jesus our Lord, in whom we have boldness and access with confidence through faith in Him." ~Ephesians 3:10-12 NKJV

14 Reasons to Pray in the Holy Spirit

About a year ago I got a revelation while waiting patiently in the teller line at the bank. I approached the teller when my turn came, and he said, "How's your day treating you?" In that instance I immediately recognized how significant that question was and how crucial how I answered was. I replied, "My day is treating me exactly how I ordered it to this morning in prayer." I continued, "I don't allow the day to treat or offer me what it desires but I align my day according to God's divine order first thing every morning by speaking what I will see and experience in that day." I know that was a lot, and probably blew the bank tellers mind (or he just thought I was crazy), but the enemy loves to send us opportunities to speak contrary to faith. When we are not prepared or equipped with God's word for answers we will answer like any other person waiting to complete a transaction that does not know Jesus but is simply allowing the day to dictate their destiny. Our destiny is set, it is written, and we must war for it... DAILY.

Every day is a blessing. Every day we must enforce the victory we already have. Each day we must put principalities, powers, rulers of darkness, and spiritual hosts of wickedness in heavenly places...in their place. The word of God shares in Matthew 6:34(b) AMPC, ...Sufficient for each day is its own trouble. Therefore, if we just get comfortable with the blessing of the day and choose not to war (and I'd say early before the busy-ness of the day begins - before we leave our homes) we will welcome whatever the day offers. When we do this, we'll find ourselves warring midday - frustrated, distracted, upset with others, and in the night season un-equipped with feelings of defeat along with the deception that we are powerless. SO NOT TRUE!

There is an adversary (who is real) called the devil who presents death - instead of life, cursing - instead of blessing to those whom he may. His time is short on this earth and his strategies to get the born-again believer out of faith are at a rapid high. We are admonished in 1 Peter 5:8 (NKJV), "Be sober, be vigilant; because your adversary the devil walks about like a roaring lion, seeking whom he may devour." This means that there are some he won't even bother. I'm pretty sure it's those who put him and his cohorts in their place early each day and give him no room throughout their day or night season. Basically, it's those who are not ignorant of his device's. Those who have chosen not to just sit around and wait for trouble, but those who will use their God-given dominion, authority, and power of words to enforce what Jesus has already done on our behalf (I John 3:8).

<u>It's time to war in the spirit of Elijah and Jehu!</u>
He will also go before Him in the spirit and power of Elijah, 'to turn the hearts of the fathers to the children,' and the disobedient to the wisdom of the just, to make ready a people prepared for the Lord." Luke 1:17 NKJV

God's anointing upon Elijah changed an entire nation even during darkness. We must understand that when we war (specifically in the Spirit) we intercede not only for our lives, but also for the destiny of others. Elijah was used by God to war and prepare the way, just like John the Baptist, for the coming of our Lord and Savior Jesus the Christ – the soon coming King. <u>His 'obedience' was key to fulfilling his destiny and paving the way for others to fulfill theirs.</u> God's fire comes with His anointing and Elijah warred out of the fire of God. We are anointed and when we war we release the fire of God to demolish anything burning or stirring up that's not like God or Heaven. Jehu destroyed Jezebel and Ahab – rebellious spirits that attempted to overthrow and destroy prophets and remove their kingship. These spirits linger with the assignment of destroying true prophets sent by God to establish the kingdom wherever they have been positioned – home, workplace, business, and/or a ministry.

We are victors in battle.
It is ignorant for us to ever think we do not need to war (that's straight forward but it's the truth). We only have to evaluate the evidence of not warring for the victory to see the foolishness of that. A few examples of the result of not warring are: persistent physical symptoms; constant lack of financial resources; people increasingly not

understanding you; sudden accidents; temptations to draw back; the disrespect of children; deceit in the workplace; and immoral thoughts that just come out of nowhere without immediate rebuke... just to name a few.

Satan is the god of this world, but greater is He that is in us than he that is in this world. We have the Holy Spirit living in us. We are citizens of Heaven and temporary residents here on this earth. Don't forget that, the best is yet to come... for real. We are already winners, conquerors, and overcomers but we are encouraged to fight the good fight of faith - which means <u>we still need to fight.</u> God's word is our weapon, and the Holy Spirit reminds us that we are victors in this battle.

When we war daily, it changes how we respond to people and situations. Our responses will be fueled by wisdom and not fueled by 'the moment' or 'a feeling'. These types of responses can be regretful. When we war and order our day it changes how we are affected by any test of faith that may come. Warring will not eliminate test(s) of faith. Warring will prepare us to handle the test in faith while remaining in God's peace. It is very possible for us to experience peace every day and for peace to be still around us. We create that space. We create what we allow to be in our space. Peace or frustration? I choose peace. What about you? This place of perpetual peace is called dwelling in that secret place (Psalm 91:1) even amid a chaotic world. Once again, we are victors in this battle. Christ has the victory, which means we have the victory. We are one with Him. His victories are ours, and He has conquered for us that our Father in Heaven can receive the glory here on this earth.

<u>Pray in the Spirit when you don't know what to pray/say or how-to war using God's word.</u>
"Likewise, the Spirit also helps in our weaknesses. For we do not know what we should pray for as we ought, but the Spirit Himself makes intercession for us with groanings which cannot be uttered. Now He who searches the hearts knows what the mind of the Spirit is, because He makes intercession for the saints according to the will of God." Romans 8:26-27 NKJV

14 Reasons to Pray in the Holy Spirit

We must settle our emotions and open our spiritual eyes 'wider'- giving no room nor a place for the devil. This fight must be taken more seriously. If we are warring and we have sin in our lives (hate in our hearts, and evil thoughts of others in our minds) our warring will not produce the peace and victory expected. The root of the nature just mentioned is unbelief. Unbelief is sin. We must ask God to forgive us of any unbelief and get back to warring effectively (Mark 11:22-25). Yes, we are equipped to do so.

So, remember, our war is not with people only – because the devil will use people... it's also, with evil spirits, and fiery darts sent, and deployed to TRY and draw us from the faith we have received. The thoughts that come to the mind are the greatest platform for the enemy's playground. If we do not tear down and deal with thoughts that speak death (not life), the door to the enemy will remain open and His evil spirits will be assigned to wreak havoc in our lives, marriages, family, business, relationships, and/or ministry. It's up to us to REBUKE 'feelings' of heaviness, oppression, and or depression and deal with our minds. We are admonished not to allow our hearts to be troubled as well (John 14:1) ...this is instruction from God. He IS NOT telling us He will do it, it's up to us. We 'choose' to keep our minds girded/guarded with the Truth and to war as victors in this battle. WE WIN AGAIN!

Finally, my brethren, be strong in the Lord and in the power of His might. Put on the whole armor of God, that you may be able to stand against the wiles of the devil. For we do not wrestle against flesh and blood, but against principalities, against powers, against the rulers of the darkness of this age, against spiritual host of wickedness in the heavenly places. Therefore, take up the whole armor of God, that you may be able to withstand in the evil day, and having done all, to stand. Stand therefore, having girded your waist with truth, having put on the breastplate of righteousness, and having shod your feet with the preparation of the gospel of peace; above all, taking the shield of faith with which, you will be

able to quench all the fiery darts of the wicked one. And take the helmet of salvation, and the sword of the Spirit, which is the word of God; praying always with all prayer and supplication in the Spirit, being watchful to this end with all perseverance and supplication for all the saints. Ephesians 6:10-18 NKJV

Love,
Tracy

14 Reasons to Pray in the Holy Spirit

PRAYER TO REPENT & TURN TO GOD

Acts 26:20b... that they should repent [change their inner self—their old way of thinking] and turn to God, doing deeds and living lives which are consistent with repentance.

14 Reasons to Pray in the Holy Spirit

Romans 10:8-10... But what does it say? "The word is near you, in your mouth and in your heart" (that is, the word of faith which we preach): that if you confess with your mouth the Lord Jesus and believe in your heart that God has raised Him from the dead, you will be saved. For with the heart one believes unto righteousness, and with the mouth confession is made unto salvation.

Now, with your faith increased to receive salvation (to be born again and have a new life in Christ) by the reading of this book and the above referenced scriptures from the word of God please take time right now to read the following prayer out loud, loud enough for your own ears to hear it:

Father God, I repent, and I turn from all my wicked ways to serve Jesus Christ as my Lord and my Savoir. I know in my heart and I confess with my mouth that You rose Jesus from the dead and He is now seated at Your right hand in heavenly places. I declare by my confession of faith, by the blood of Jesus, and by Your grace God, I am saved - I am born again - and I receive eternal life in Jesus name, amen!

> Next step: Ask God to lead you to a sound, Bible teaching, spirit-filled ministry that will disciple you and teach you how to walk by faith and not by sight.
>
> *"For we walk by faith, not by sight.*
> *2 Corinthians 5:7*
>
> *"But without faith it is impossible to please Him, for he who comes to God must believe that He is, and that He is a rewarder of those who diligently seek Him.*
> *Hebrews 11:6*

14 Reasons to Pray in the Holy Spirit

Prayer in the Spirit is a sign of obedience and a yielded heart.

This act of faith is sure to make the will of God tangible in our lives.

Tracy L. Williams

14 Reasons to Pray in the Holy Spirit

PRAYER TO RECEIVE THE GIFT OF THE HOLY SPIRIT

Acts 8:14-17... When the apostles in Jerusalem heard that [the people of] Samaria had accepted the word of God, they sent Peter and John to them. They came down and prayed for them that they might receive the Holy Spirit; for He had not

yet fallen on any of them; they had simply been baptized in the name of the Lord Jesus [as His possession]. Then Peter and John laid their hands on them [one by one], and they received the Holy Spirit.

Mark 11:24... For this reason, I am telling you, whatever you ask for in prayer, believe (trust and be confident) that it is granted to you, and you will (get it)." AMPC

As a minister of the gospel of Jesus Christ, I pray, in the name of Jesus, that you receive the gift of the Holy Spirit the moment you believe and receive while declaring (reading) the following prayer... out loud:

Dear Heavenly Father, I come to You in the name of Jesus, and I desire to be baptized with Your Holy Spirit with the evidence of speaking in other tongues. Your word says that I can have it, and I believe what You have said. I receive this gift by faith in Jesus' name. I thank You, Father, that I am baptized with the Holy Spirit with the evidence of speaking in other tongues!

But you, beloved, build yourselves up (founded) on your most holy faith (make progress, rise like an edifice higher and higher), praying in the Holy Spirit. ~Jude 1:20

14 Reasons to Pray in the Holy Spirit

PRAYER LIFE...
ENCOURAGES DAILY COMMUNICATION WITH GOD.

PRAYER LIFE...
LAUNCHES PRAYER WARRIORS TO THEIR NEXT LEVEL.

PRAYER LIFE...
CAUSES BOLDNESS AND ERADICATES FEAR.

PRAYER LIFE...
BIRTHS INTERCESSORS WHO UNDERSTAND GOD'S HEART. ALL BY DECLARING GOD'S WORD WITH...

14 Reasons to Pray in the Holy Spirit

Tracy L. Williams

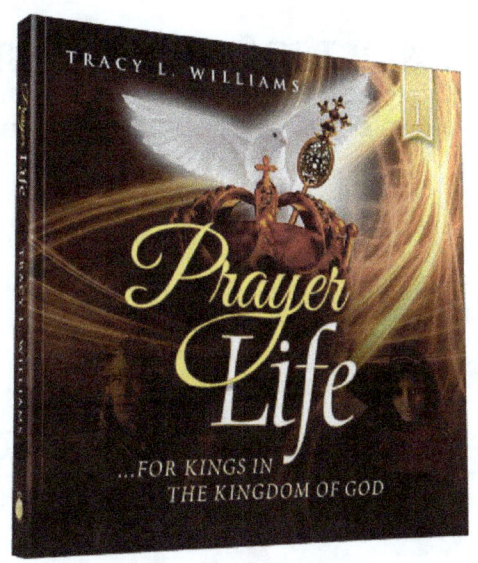

Prayer Life (book & teaching series)
by Tracy L. Williams
tlwpublications.com

CONTACT TRACY L. WILLIAMS

For more info and/or the purchase of books:

tlwpub@icloud.com (email)
tlwpublications.com (website)

TLW Publications
PO Box 1413
Claremont, CA 91711

STAY CONNECTED WITH TRACY:

Instagram
@mrs.tracy

2 – Channels
Tracy L. Williams & Prayer Life

www.ingramcontent.com/pod-product-compliance
Lightning Source LLC
Chambersburg PA
CBHW052025290426
44112CB00014B/2376